KU-016-704

Sloth Yoga™

Published by Willow Creek Press, Inc.
P.O. Box 147, Minocqua, Wisconsin 54548

Design: Donnie Rubo
Printed in China

Sloth Yoga™

WILLOW CREEK PRESS®

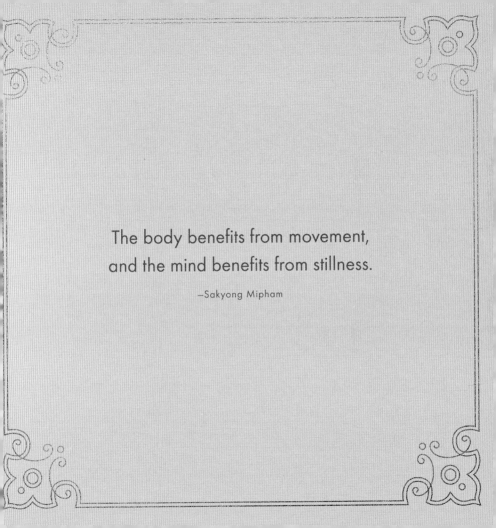

The body benefits from movement,
and the mind benefits from stillness.

—Sakyong Mipham

Your soul is your best friend. Treat it with care,
nurture it with growth, feed it with love.

—Ashourina Yalda

Have only love in your heart for others.
The more you see the good in them, the
more you will establish good in yourself.

—Paramahansa Yogananda

Inhale the future. Exhale the past.

—Unknown

Yoga begins right where I am—not where I was yesterday or where I long to be.

—Linda Sparrowe

I have been a seeker and I still am, but
I stopped asking the books and the stars.
I started listening to the teaching of my Soul.

—Rumi

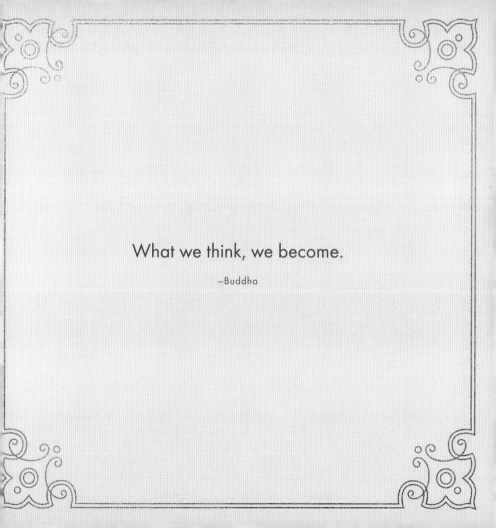

What we think, we become.

—Buddha

A river cuts through a rock, not because
of its power, but its persistence.

—Unknown

There are many goals but one path—
the path of compassion.

—Amit Ray

Happiness is not a matter of intensity but of balance, order, rhythm and harmony.

—Thomas Merton

Have wisdom in your actions
and faith in your merits.

—Yogi Bhajan

Yoga is like music. The rhythm of the body, the melody of the mind, and the harmony of the soul create the symphony of life.

—B.K.S. Iyengar

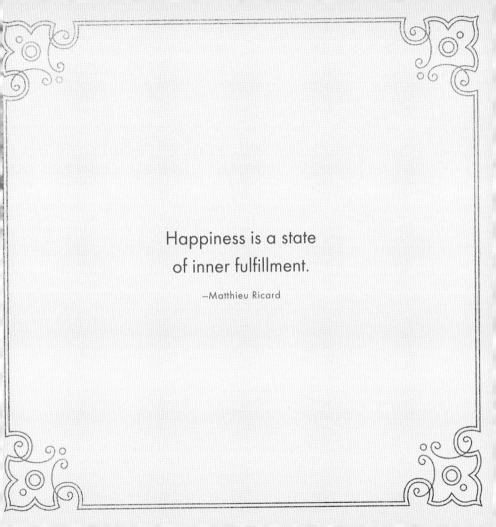

Happiness is a state
of inner fulfillment.

—Matthieu Ricard

The wise man lets go of all results, whether good or bad, and is focused on the action alone.

—Bhagavad Gita

Sometimes you find yourself in the middle of nowhere, and sometimes in the middle of nowhere, you find yourself.

—Unknown

Blessed are the flexible, for they
shall not be bent out of shape.

—Unknown

When the mind is exhausted
of images, it invents its own.

—Gary Snyder

In our uniquely human capacity of connect movement with breath and spiritual meaning, yoga is born.

—Gurmukh Kaur Khalsa

In the midst of movement and chaos,
keep stillness inside of you.

—Deepak Chopra

Our bodies are our gardens to
which our wills are gardeners.

—William Shakespeare

Peace comes from within.
Do not seek it without.

—Buddha

You must find the place inside yourself
where nothing is impossible.

—Deepak Chopra

The body is your temple. Keep it pure
and clean for the soul to reside in.

—B.K.S. Iyengar

The part can never be well
unless the whole is well.

—Plato

Silence is not silent. Silence speaks. It speaks most eloquently. Silence is not still. Silence leads. It leads most perfectly.

—Sri Chinmoy

Sitting quietly, doing nothing, spring comes,
and the grass grows by itself.

—Zen Proverb

You cannot travel the path until
you have become the path itself.

—Buddha

Be a lamp to yourself. Be your
own confidence. Hold to the truth
within yourself as to the only truth.

—Buddha

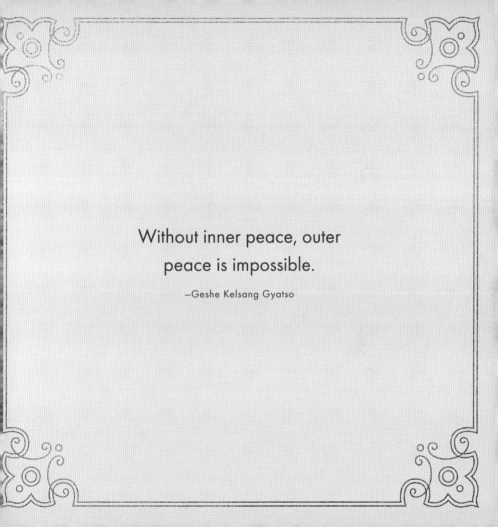

Without inner peace, outer peace is impossible.

—Geshe Kelsang Gyatso

Mindfulness helps you go home to the present. And every time you go there and recognize a condition of happiness that you have, happiness comes.

—Thich Nhat Hanh

There is no need for temples, no need for complicated philosophies. My brain and my heart are my temples; my philosophy is kindness.

—Dalai Lama

Your task is not to seek for love, but merely
to seek and find all the barriers within
yourself that you have built against it.

—Rumi

Sun salutations can energize and
warm you, even on the darkest,
coldest winter day.

—Carol Krucoff

When you find peace within yourself, you
become the kind of person who
can live at peace with others.

—Peace Pilgrim